XULECA LOUNGE

poems by
Kevin Clifford Burke

XULECA LOUNGE
Poems by
Kevin Clifford Burke

First Paperback edition, 2022.
Printed in the United States of America
ISBN: 978-0-578-96364-8
Library of Congress Control Number: 2022901314

For more information on the author, please visit his website:
KCliffordBurke.com

Published by
Amazon Kindle Direct Publishing
Amazon Digital Services LLC
410 Terry Avenue North
Seattle, WA 98109
KDP.Amazon.com/en_US/

To Miguel, who makes me happy and has always loved and believed in me, challenging me to give my best and to me, for writing this book wherein lies the blood of my soul. I earned it and gave it my all.

Table of Contents

Foreward

I always say a poet walks a lonely path. They are the monks of the literary world, solitary devotees of a unique Holy Trinity - rhyme, scheme and meter.

The poet also worships words, and uses them with care and cunning and caution. They are exacting with syllables, obsessed with imagery, and fascinated by symbolism. Basically, they love language, and suffer, because of this, a lifelong journey to find - whenever they sit down to write – just the 'right line'.

Kevin Burke, to this definition, is a poet. A really good one. His work springs from a boundless fountain of energy and ambition, feeling and determination to put on the page exactly what he's feeling in his heart. And he has a big heart.

I met Kevin years ago, through work, and after a bit of getting to know you moments, we came to share those dreaded three words between people of the pen – "You write too?" And with that confirmation, we began to build a friendship that included, among other positive and affirming elements, a mutual respect for each other's work, for art, and unrelenting support for our creative projects, whatever they may be (Kevin is also is an accomplished singer and guitarist).

And so I'm here, in this moment, to give my complete backing to *Xuleca Lounge*, Kevin's latest gift of poetry. The book follows his two earlier collections: first, *Angry June Moon Says Hello* (2009), one of the most eloquent, vivid and truthful accounts of the pain, frustration, and ultimate joy of "coming out" as a gay person, and then *The Bridge of Love* (2011), filled with gorgeous, soul-bursting verse about fulfilment in a romantic relationship and how it impacts on how life is seen and experienced from a contented and ebullient heart.

Now we have *Xuleca Lounge*. The title comes from the first poem, as sensuous a piece I have ever read, a mix of flavors and beats and mind-twisting questions and affirmations, a delight for the contrarian and those seeking answers to life's questions. Kevin fills the rest of the pages with poems that connect back to themes in his past books, but push forward to a more mature and wiser look back and forward. He has evolved, as a person, and a writer.

I'll end with some advice for the reader, given to me by a wonderful poet about reading poetry. To paraphrase, he said, "Don't read all the poems at once. Read them like you would view a painting at an art museum. Taking time to really study the work. Even going back to review again, until, finally, the totality of the piece sets in."
And so I say grab your glass of wine, or a soothing tea or whatever sipping beverage delights you, and start with poem one. Take your time. And give yourself to the work. Trust me, it's worth the investment.

John McCaffrey, Author of Two Syllable Men, June 2021

Preface

I suppose there are many reasons why one writes. For me, it has often been an explosive affair where the overflow of emotion and vision demand to be scribbled onto the blank page until it finished with you! You don't know what you are going to say or whether anything you've written makes any sense; however, trusting in your creative talent and the voice of the unconscious, you give way to their powers. Then there is the mundane part of surveying what you've written, making sense of what was written and then crafting and obsessing over the piece until it is 'finished'. Of course, finished is a very relative term that is like being in a thousand consecutive Plato's caves. After you think you've crafted the true vision of what the poem is about, you then see beyond it to a truer and better version of what the poem's vision is 'really' about, and so on. The trick is not to destroy the original idea but to honor it, to let it lead you to what it's really meant to be, like a block of marble that tells the sculptor what it wants to be. But like the analogy of Plato's cave, writing is always about truth: one's inner truth and what one actually sees. This book of mine was a truly demanding master wanting to be tamed with much clarity and crafting of that truth. It drew much blood, unforgiving until that truth had been finally revealed. I don't say the book is perfect but, as far as I'm concerned, it is finished! If I may say so, there is enough truth in it to last for a while.

The idea of the title poem began in a dream I had when my husband and I were visiting a favorite city of ours, Philadelphia, one Fourth of July weekend back in 2009, two years before we were married. In the dream, I encountered Xuleca Lounge, a space that I could go to and feel inspired to wonder at the edge of the creative process. There was some contention in the dream over the title of the poem. Someone claimed the idea and title was theirs; but I knew it was my idea since in the dream I had already created and owned it! When I awoke, I wrote down the dream and so the poem began to germinate and tell my story about this special portal to go to when one wants to create: a place I believe we all may visit for solitude's creativity, love, loss... and rebirth.

Included in this book are poems about the search for solitude, for God (a life-long journey), for love, for my father, my sense of self, and the celebration of my marriage to my husband. The book also contains what I have come to call my poetics of trauma poems regarding memories of abandonment, abuse and dissociation. Although their subject matter is difficult, they contain things that awakened me to, and thus helped me deal with realities I initially might not have seen until I started to write about them. Poems and writing in general, can speak to us of the past and present, helping us clarify and make sense of things. Doing the work of writing helps the writer share these visions with the reader. For me, this is the power of words. Like music, they can give voice to the ordinary and ineffable and put them within our reach. Words can teach us what our voice is, how to use them and how to make them sing, if we are willing to listen and do the work. They must reflect or mirror our experience... like a pool of water rippling with the wind.

This brings me to gratefully acknowledge the generosity of three writers who were kind enough to read my book and offer their praise and feedback. To Martin Keefe, thank you for your beautiful summary that is on the back cover of this book. And much thanks to Howard J. Kogan and John McCaffrey, who have always believed in me as a writer and supported me in my journey to find my voice. Their writing has inspired me with their exquisite use of words as well as in their comments and feedback. Howard, the eagle-eyed poet, who, with understated simplicity and clarity, was quick to point out with a word or two or a question about whether things made sense or not. He also lent his hand as we worked together on the opening stanzas of the poem, Museum. John challenged me to finish this project. You see, we both had an agreement to finish our books a while ago. He would finish the novel he was working on and I, this book. And voila, here we are! I do hope you will take the opportunity to read all three of these writers' works.

Kevin Clifford Burke, July 2021

Xuleca Lounge

I gazed upon
the snowcapped Andes
floating clouds that loomed
craggéd ledges razor sharp,
the silent sultry noon.

I yearned for the heavens
over legions of peaks
like layers of cloudy wreaths
doubts defused, then marooned.

Still, I prefer quiet serenity,
in a restful alleyway in Mexico City
and a mid-morning tune
as I await the opening day
shaded from the misty haze
of bruised hope and burnt ruin
and the dream of transcendence
consumed.

Now I love Philly's
tree-tempered shadowed sun
where the Fourth of July was launched
before the fireworks had begun.
Crowds of families celebrate
shimmering pinwheels, clusters of stars
flares shot from the smoking gun...
the revolution's sign of Mars.

→

Xuleca Lounge
Xuleca Lounge
from a dream came your name and sound
slow longing's labor
seeds planted, fertile ground
a respite from chattering
to temper the magical realm.
At café tables you are seated
to drink beneath the breezing elms.

Xuleca Lounge
Xuleca Lounge
a place I invented,
and loved unbound
though love's lost thread did abscond
to leave you searching for this pearl
with great abound.
For isn't this where
the value of time
can really be found?
So take time and wait.
Listen for the heart's quiet sound
where the latent wonder of silence lives,
waiting to serve its heavenly round.

Xuleca Lounge
Xuleca Lounge
eternity suspended
in the skies and on the ground,
your invisible refreshment lifts us

always soothing time
with its
caressing
silent
beckoning
balm.

Love's Bliss

When I awake,
I stumble out of my twilight state.
Dreams interrupted,
smear and brake
unconscious affairs of love and hate.
The Id's fountain issues forth its copious spate.
Kaleidoscopic images, meanderings employ
their metaphorical bait.
A glimpse of insight to enjoy
through chaos' fears,
that may be a clue towards
revelation's joys and tears.
Captivating musings
come upon my tongue tripping
on a wishful vision buoyed
while good and evil angels dance entwined
and never fail to cross my logic's line.

Still…
music floats
upon the far reaches of the sea,
waves' haunting swells and sighs
tell you to put away
your clumsy strides and be,
like the stuttering you might make before you fly.
Eyes closed wide,
angels dance across the heavens bright and sing.

Bachian viols and cellos swing.
Guitar canyons strung,
rasgueodos like lightning strummed
praise the open abyss.
The moon hid its Blakean stare
behind its sacred mists
until you opened your soul
like a sunflower
to the music of the sun and wind's kiss
and dared…

Ruffling his hair in the silent crotch
of flamboyant earth masculine surprise,
once forbidden
until I awoke one morning
and he took me into his arms
with our tongues to kiss
soul tried and probing
our love's bliss.

Waiting for Sunrise

The dark hollow of niches
enlivened by the full moon's light
empty but for the concrete warmth of the lunar lamp
the shadows of windswept moving trees bright.

My spirit wanders amid these
buildings of stone,
Spanish tiled slate
while I, cycling past Garden City mansions
and Garrison's castles,
search for a place to rest,
in a quiet darkened grove of pines alone.

I pray to the air of the forests,
the arbor's midday light
that seeps through the gray-green branches
of sheltered woods.
My footsteps powdering the dirt
of stone-strewn paths
while I seek to lose all and be lost
in your solitude and fullness.

Birds circle and flit from branch and limb,
their piping songs and calls do echo
through the forest glade
like a pastoral or dream.

As I wait for your voice
to come like a consuming fire
which lives and gives life
in all that I've seen.

The river runs long:
from Manhattan Island North
to the Bear Mountain Bridge and West Point,
where giant colonial chains once
spread out across the river
to block the British ships.

I cannot breathe in the air
suffocating from the pain,
deep within.

Solitude's Hour

Let our voices rise to the skies
dear transcendental one,
Creator, respondent to all our whys??!!
Eternal incumbent filing for us
with all of His cloudy briefs
echoing the crowd's dance,
mugging for our attention,
singing silently, laughing
filled with compassion against all our horrors
and our shouting from above and below.
If you hear me, please...give a holler!
Please, stop by and say hello.

My thorny crown is killing me.
I'm soaked in the dried blood of brown,
delicately framing my thoughts
for the next unanswerable question
as I tread water tirelessly,
afraid of falling beneath the water's surface...
one last time.

Oh, why can't I separate from my sadness of dour brown
so that I don't drown and swim?
Can't seem to wade away from the living
hell or smile, even clown.
Can't put out the melting candles before
they burn the tablecloth brown.

Wax is dripping all over the white lace;
the candle is supported in my bare hand now,
pure sparks of green and sulfur smells
It's a masochistic game…
matches struck against my wooden frame.

I suppose I'm game now for
trying another way with myself
to avoid all of this sadness
as your mother slowly dies from the inside.
I can't bear to think of it and yet it's
the only way it could go,
her smiling in her wheelchair,
mumbling incoherently to herself
to the side of the wall.
I suppose you won't hear none of it
no more – that'll fix it!
As my head vibrates from this internal brawl
banging against the wall of death you fear
a wall connecting you and her...
or nothing at all.

You had the last word.
Did you think I could let it go by?
I wandered so long to hear it,
I wanted so much to cry,
raise my voice
and shout with all the others
to put in my two cents.
I hope this is making sense.

Each day I pray you'll hear my cry.
But I've run out of incense.
Can't make it to the sacraments.
All I've left is me.
It's all I'm allowed.
It's all that I can be.

Now I long for the lovely ecstasy of improvisation,
melody twining the heaven's dewy branches,
the arbor's opening doors.
I hope I am not late for the solitude's hour
whose waves are lapping against the shore of heaven's door
when shadows and lights play in the hills
and the blades of grass attend to the shades
of true silent prayer.

I hope I am not too late to partake
of this momentous communion
commingling
beyond all time and knowledge.
I bask, lay my head and rest
upon its sweet lullaby of green
I cannot wonder
I must only wait with joyous expectation
greeting the aridity of hope
that floods the day.

Sleigh Ride

My bones feel stretched
like parched ironed shirts
overworn, tired and wretched,
hung out to dry on a wire
like a relic, fitted for a museum
starched of all desire.

This is my reward
for speaking too often out of turn,
a gay foppish bard
playing the fun-loving fool,
giving himself away for free
ashamed his soul could ever be
like some bright shining jewel.

While dead,
someone dragged me into my coffin.
The priests planned more murders wanton
as the sarcophagus lid was left open.
Someone then stole my mummy,
sacrificed for worshipping Aton.
And so, I remained a lover of the sun
while I looked for a place on the beach
and searched for the horizon
longing for someone to come with me,
my fears allay,
discourse on the setting sunlight

→

I keep on trying to fight
as I try to put aside
the dying of the light
for the clothes of the day.

Wandering further I finally lay
my head and my ear on the ground
the source that my soul longs to hear
the rippling waves of water
quiet reflecting sound
the firm beach beneath my body
serves as my unshrinking bed
away from the terrors of the highway
in a gliding speeding hyper-blinding
hyperbolic sled.

Celluloid Snowfall

Celluloid snowfall
dull sheen shiny shades
an airbrushed whitened
streak darkened into a pall
of coagulated blood
and a fagotty catcall.

Cold snow melts
before it finally fades
whiteness ruined by
monochromatic smoky grays
the suicidal self-editing swath
creates the self-splicing blade.

Beaconed memories, hidden mists
upon the fluorescent screen laid.
Now I reach out to soothe the toddler,
once standing tall.
I learned early not to make a scene
to avoid the maddening rage and snow,
practicing not to fall.

An uneasy sigh,
a clarion call
in anxious flight
I tried to climb past
your voluminous gaze of ice on a wall

in broad daylight.
Shaken repudiation,
you dressed me down
made me feel terror and small.
Still, I longed to dress tall
in your petticoats of angelic swirling gauze
and celluloid snowfall.

The blurring film is
focused now
violent and silent
the shock of derisive laughter
left me stubborn,
cowering in freedom,
embarrassment's shame
failing to climb over their wall.
So, I clung to a land of shadows
exiled and in flight
hallows, ambivalent and contrite
childhood's magical innocence shunned
for a land of sanctimonium
and a growing taste for Catholic martyrdom.
Introibo ad altare Deum
desperate to approach the altar of saints.
In exchange for holiness,
I will trade in my sight against temptation's feints.

Of celluloid snow
obscuring
the memory

of fate and longing.
Celluloid film
spinning in my mind
running, never belonging
entangled and blind.
Celluloid snowfall
is always my downfall
so I'll never remember my lines.
Can't win a leading role
in my motion picture, I cried,
The healing is wounded
Though unstaunched,
I feel like the bleeding is occluded
when celluloid snowfall remains denied.

Conflagration

Out of my dreams
came the fire of the sun
my helpless seams
in annihilation
my dying self
set ablaze
a high-flying Phoenix
burst the ashes' conflagration
I flew out of the Minotaur's maze
my pathway undetected
a new being resurrected
conflict's lightning undone
the past eschewed
a god indestructible
I became renown.
I was renewed.

But... this Icarus fell,
webbed wax falling
through ashes dispelled.
Wildly blown and scattered,
the four winds were soaring.

Now I spend my time redrawing
new patterns with new means
re-stitch, repair my ragged cloaks,
clawing through my battered tears

that only failure brings
to rearrange my color's constructions
and broken tired wings;
become someone new,
build a better dream.

As the sky cried,
through the empty hollow of blue,
and falling dripping wings...
the Phoenix spoke these words anew:
"Your wings, like pleasant pipedreams
were made to dissolve like the fallen rain.
With each step you take
they begin to evaporate
though your journey had just begun.
They melt like wax and break
when you edge too near the sun."

"How can I endure the star's burning stare?
How do I fashion stronger wings
to beat the sun-glazed air?
Wings not made to be swallowed
as sunlight reveals its
heaven challenging dare."

Where do I go when slipping from a trapeze
suspended in mid-air?
The stakes below uprooted,
the sagging net, another scare.

Then I made my leap to confound,
streaming tear's regrets
the audience silenced with its bets,
hushed momentarily without a sound
their tiny stares and open mouths
now staring up at this clown
I fell...
far, far below
unhinged and crashing
onto the ground.

Poseidon
(New Year's Waltz)

The lamp rays
ascend
the warm lit ceiling
ensconced, beaming
(I was)
without a sound
boundless
soundless
resounding
conceiving.

The clock is ticking
a midnight pulse,
an unrelenting
staccato waltz
I lay here watchful,
a sorrowful
electric seer
on the eve
of a new year.

Clouds of the sky god come
to envelop our horizon:
fiery black across a darkening sky.

→

Poseidon's waves thrown in the air
crystallizing shapes of fear.
His ominous trident threatening
throat-aimed spear,
past the Pleiades'
black expanse,
tripling his growing throne's
endless remonstrance.
From his height and depths
we watch the earth
covered by the sea
tonight in this echo of darkness
from the hollow of a cave
I flee...

The fantasy of a bend
where terror does lay
hidden behind
my heart's escarpment
tripped upon each day.

I ran from
the maddening figure
throttling my throat,
his erected member,
high-priced touch,
sparking under age
clawing hands,
bartered clutch

broken,
a child
in invisible death
awash.

Grasping an illicit key,
towards a jarred open door.
Terror's freedom
drawn from once
unknown
forgotten shores.

Before the Door of Nothingness

In Huntington, in the living room, of my grandparents'
house upon the black convertible sofa, I slept…

Before the door of nothingness
I lay awake, unable to sleep
bored in the cloudy morning's
dark twilight so, so, so deep,
I cannot rest.
I cannot fight.
I am alone… on a couch I do not own
in a stygian starless room of night
gripped with palpable fear
and paralysis so, so tight.

I cannot move
strangled by fear's outstretched iron claw;
stung
into helpless submission;
wrung
like a twisted rag,
feeling and tears dried out,
I couldn't command any words to come forth.
I couldn't cry for help;
nor, could I in terror shout.

Nothing feels too dear.
All that was not wrung out
was the hiding invisible fear.

Lost in the Language of X-Rays

Alone in a cyclone
between light and dark zones:
crackling film
pierced by impregnable light
I moan.
Horrors wrest me from the fight
caught within the corners of plastic film tight
petrified in the blight
vulnerable to exposure
I stalk the lost cause of fears
exposed in tears.
Hoping for a reawakening
that never comes.
Dilapidated rainy days falsely phased
I'm lost
in the language of X-rays.

Lost to colorless ways
an insidious painting of
sorrowful bays
snapped by the end of a whip
sent crashing into despair
the lost language of X-rays
gray sunsets, endless stairs.

Child blocked
the father's cock

→

numb and dim
frozen prey of vermin,
excited, repulsed
can't run away
nor remember the memories
silenced shades so dim,
so far away.

I beat my head against the door
shouting, "Open! Will you open!?"
"I know there's more knowledge stored..."
I lay perfectly still
while I run my brain waves
through the invisible opening of the portal
of transitional space.
Waiting for rapprochement
to examine the days once erased
in a plasticine one-dimensional maze
the silent fruitlessness of transparence
lost in the language of X-rays.

Climbing the Rope
To my father

Climbing the rope in 2nd grade
no effort, no net.
Next year was harder,
hoisting myself up
hand over hand.
It got harder and harder yet
without you to catch me
in case I fell.
At first I was high and laughing;
but as the years went by
I was treading water,
trapped at the bottom of a well.

I couldn't run away,
no longer wanted
by your side.
If I stayed at a distance
maybe I had it right…
as long as I didn't cry.

Though I didn't know it
I was invisible,
chained to your side,
a collar locked around my neck
in case I strayed too long,
too wide.

→

Forbidden to be by your side
or the sides of other young handsome men.
I was a brave stoic soldier
whose warm winning smile never died,
though I could see the soldier in your eyes
we both longed to love...
for our bitter sadness never lied.

Later I would find the courage
to cut the chain,
though it hurt my hands
to finally compress
the metal handled shears
in desperation deep.
Awakened out of a fearful sleep,
I was thrown
upon my forward face
flying alone, cold and crashing
flung far from centrifugal grace.
A man in space
abandoned by you
and by friends, debased.
I entered a rainbow universe,
on a search for someone new
to make my stamp upon this place.

Finally free from the cut chain then...
grafted to the music of liberation
I became liberty's scion
with terror and anxiety as close friends.

Now freed from the plaints of bondage bound:
feet planted firmly on the ground
able to fly like Mercury
with wingéd feet crowned.
Emboldened, flying,
I was found
resolute and ready
to protect myself from being spurned
against self-denigration,
feeling once again disgraced,
no longer a prisoner in a bell jar
without a sound,
without a face.

Satori of the Trees

The bus rode towards the bridge
the Verrazano not so narrow
gazing upon the tree-bedecked landscape
in reds and golds
burnished scarlet brushstrokes of clustered hanging boughs
we were steered through the day's regal crimson
through flashing revelation
brilliance burnished bold
autumn's show unfolds
within the interior forest tapestry of trees
illuminated deep within
a hallowed clearing
sunlight gentle, warmly glows.

Scuttled crimson leaves
laughing yellows draped and sallow
browns entwined upon the mottled bark bearing trunks
the tree wears her red-stained fur draped in elegance
plumage of dried plum
plumage of the arbor's Phoenix
plumage of the fall
within the dying light
the Indian summer's sun
who gave his light to all.

Satori of the trees
flight of the seasons

forsaking their zenith
after the ascension of orgasm
and the loss of love that weepeth
you refuse to meet
so cherished and yet...
so bittersweet.

Red Trees

In autumn's early poignant light
the clarity of morning is unconcealed;
and the sky, like the rings of Saturn, is filled
with pale salmons, gun-metal blues
and golds.

Before the early evening's
twilight aging sighs:
the transformation of once verdant greenery
vibrantly breathing
into the blazing
of yellow, orange and red trees
is realized.

Here the fading vision
is finally recognized:
amid blazing red trees
and palely lit
ascending red skies.

Songs from the Secret Garden

Morning comes.
The trees and grass are darkly shaped
in the morning dew.
I believe in resurrection's secret
sweet silent breezy songs
secretly sung
in a garden,
sweetly sung,
with you.

How can I contain them?
Teach myself to remember their words?
They trip off my soul
and vanish,
leaving imprints so bold,
I cannot live without them
once caressed by your presence
I am graced to hold
once they've spoken their melodies,
once they've spoken through the trees,
once our spirits have been dancing:
together, just you and me.

→

I believe in resurrection
of love's sweet silent breezy songs
sung forever in tune;
in a secret garden
sung forever
with you.

Rain Poem

I love to listen to the falling rain
slashing upon the outside.
See the swaying branches,
soaked and bending
beneath the water's weight.
Trees, blown by the wind,
as the rain bounces off our roof-tops
quicksilver-like
and quickly told to brake.

I love to listen to the rain
its incessant drizzling sweet sustain
slushing the earth's palette
with a shapeless pouring mallet,
quelling thirsting clay and plants
glistening with animals, insects and ants.
Making mirrors out of streets
and soggy rags out of
hanging laundry sheets.

I love to listen to the rain
amid thunder's drums
pounding out their rhythms
behind a midnight train,
its lonely fleeting whistle
muted by warm summer winds.

$\longrightarrow$

Behind the distant mountain's echoes...
it echoes once again.
Now water pours down
upon lengthening shadows
coloring the branches
of dying autumn
with glistening gray.

I love to listen to the falling rain,
silently sober
soberly tamed
by the gentle softness of its plasticity,
despite being a placated plaintiff
against autumn's rusticity
and this cloudy subsistence of the fall.
I will miss the glad walking days
expectant with golden-particled rays
filled with dark summer's sadness,
of the forested late morning sun.
Still... I will listen to the calming rain
on this silent gray day.

But when I see the vanishing of each raindrop,
perchance, a bathing sparrow spot,
I will then bask in the silence
of a rainbow's prism and stop
my cloud-filled meandering.

The Fall Show

The fall show is over:
lawns of fallen, trampled leaves
left to the drifting chance
of a damp chilly autumn breeze.

So we left the city in our cars
escaping to the country
bleeding, maced and marred
our apartment hallways crammed
in crowded subways,
subterranean tunnels jammed
spurned beneath the heavens
in early mornings and early nights,
the jobs of our thoughts
our mortgaged lives
inhaled with regret contrite.

The fall show is over
and it has scraped and scrapped
every tree and pavement
leaving peeling potholed scars
beneath smooth scabless trees
lining every house and street
as we drive, our tires rambling rattling
the treacherous domain
my numbing confusion's enfeebling daemon
no longer able to really know

$\longrightarrow$

the naked rush of a sun's shadow;
herein this year lies the end of the fall show.

The fall show is over
for lawns of fallen, trampled leaves
left only to the drifting chance
of a damp chilly autumn breeze.

Parades she upon the spot-lit dais,
pausing in each pose and seasonal mood
smiling, dressed in red sequins and shoes.
Ah! She is dressed like a jewel,
glittering in the spotlight bright
waiting for applause
she sashays across the stage
back and forth she goes
brightly colored like the fall spread of leaves
she parades on
and then off she goes.
Another willowing figure waves,
for the crowd to know
there's just no end to the next dress
that dazzles one
at the fall show.
Like brightly colored spread leaves
she parades and sways,
then off she goes.

The fall show is over
for lawns of fallen, trampled leaves

left only to the drifting chance
of a damp chilly autumn breeze.

The willow's sequins have fallen.
I'm walking now in the forest bare
to the blighting waking song,
the rustle of the crackling leaves
beneath my feet.

I hear the river's trickling song,
the sounds and speed of the wind
while listening for winter's spirit deep,
I hear whispers of the coming snows
to cover the earth before I go,
to be my mantel before I sleep.

Caribbean Colors
(before the light of day)

Rain would not wash away
Thanksgiving holiday
nor sun burn its rage into
our unprotected skins.
Stars fell not from the sky,
in the Boricuan countryside.
And the seas did not disrupt
the fortress studded beaches wide
when birds were cradled in the trees,
singing with the brightening daylight sky.

Gentle breezes cradled us too
as we ran along the beach's
breaking waves of blue.
The coqui beckoned last night
with his happy iambic tunes.
Night shades came to cloak the vigilant sun.
Arawak Taino once walked the gardens
in deep obeisance to the earth.
Swans and peacocks slept
before lidless mists of velveteen shades.
Gold fish swam in pools of gray.
They darted and they swayed
like us before the light of day.

Caribbean colors swim in the shades
and in the light of day.
When you laugh and hold my hand,
we can see our way.
The romance of the breeze
won't release us from its spell
'til we've danced beneath the clouds,
flown upon the prism's colors
before the ocean's waves,
the cradle of our dell.

I Think You Know Me

I think you know me
but I'm afraid to ask
who is the man in the mirror
wearing that half-frozen mask?
I think you know me
but I'm always afraid to ask
as I watch your fleeting figure
hiding in the shadows
wearing scared,
where you've always been and basked
balking at seeing the light of day.
I watch for you now;
I know you're there.
I know you're real
but I'm not sure of what to say
filled somehow, with all your guilt and fear.
Why don't you just tell me what you need?
Just ask...
Still, I'm only left with
the vision of your sorrowful mask.
I know where you are
and I know now you're here.
But I'm unsure of how to help,
or, if I'm up to the task.
So I keep waiting for
your appearance,

a constant awaited arrival,
like a high-flying joyful seer
so I can grab and embrace you
with my open arms of love and tears,
joyful like the father
of the prodigal son and Self.

When Will the Queen Come?

(Inspired by Ravel's *Pavane pour une infante défunte –
Pavane for a Dead Princess*, M. 19)

Who is the Queen?
And when will she come
with her regalia and cortege?
When will she flash like a sun?
Like the Phoenix reborn?
Cleanse us of all self-hatred and scorn?
When will she raise her sceptered hand
and restore nature to its rightful time?
When will she marry the crying Fisher King,
and give him a son?
When, when, when?
When the starving and bored people sing,
praying in gutters,
in the lands of famine and plague?

When will Rapunzel
let down her golden hair?
When will the golden son
climb her golden stair
to dress for the ball?
When, when, when
will he take the lands' legions in hand?
The minions await his command,
they await his glance
the wave of his gloved hand

his confident stare
gifted with vision so fair.
The kindness he will impart
is equal only to the strength
of his moral compass and heart.
When will this prince arise from the ashes of his hearth
and roll away the stone
of his self-made tomb?
When will someone help me to raise my voice and start
my road to recover my kingdom and part?
So many years were answered with a martyr's tears.
So many years spent to patch up those fears
and cure the guilt of hands that shuddered
from wearing her robes and gilded crown over my heart.
Now the returning question arrives,
beckons you forth to process, parade and sing,
"It is time, it is time to start."
Send for the queen.
Stop the rending of clothes, the smearing of ashes
time to dress the dawn with silks and brocades
time for the sun's gleam to alight in your eyes.
It is time for you to pronounce your true name
to the day, to the darkness of the hills and the skies and rise
before the twilight of all graves
and rescue one who mourns uncontrollably
for his soul, lost in the shadows of a cave
that hid him from his sacred birth
in another's grave.

It is time
to shine like the sun

wrest the light from the stars
sing freely
smiling with the aliveness of the day.
Touching your gentle hands and lips,
I feel the aliveness of your body
with my fingertips
as you hold mine in sway.
I cede command now to your armies today
so we can love, laugh and play.
And so I rise
like a sun
no longer a queen
no longer a prince
but only an heir
to the fullness of your soul and mine
before all who pass
unabashed, unashamed.
A bolero of passion,
the duende of night
the confidence of love
unrestrained
uncontrite.
No longer caught between
the shadows of the grave.
The more we shine,
know each other
and play…
in the deepening shadows of the hills
in the fullness of love and of the day.

Pavane for a Dead Daddy

Where's Daddy?
Daddy's dead.
Nowhere to be found.
Gone.
Invisible.
Sulking.
Undercover.
He doesn't want you
the way you want him.
And, yet, once he did.
So your only alternative
is to be a man
and want things
you're supposed to want:
Mommy for protection,
marry Mommy and be safe
but chained.

This mournful ballad
this curling rising pavane
for a dead princess
you were never allowed to be.
Only a prince
in the wrong hands
abandoned by him
and you,
suffering in silence

→

and confused efforts
to be a man.

No maps and no one
allowed to go inside
your locked box
with signs that say,
"Stay away."
Come closer
to the joke
who calls himself
a man
without ties.

The Song of the Fire

To Miguel, on the day of our wedding, October 15, 2011

The fire, the fire, the fire
love, hunger and desire
the flame
burning deep inside me
deep inside us
burning bright
acetylene torch
an indelible match
a tiny mustard seed
growing wild, untamed
it ravishes my body
with thoughts of you
enlivens my love
it maims
the dark desert of emptiness
landscape of darkness and chaos
the flame wrenches me free
from myself
returning us to its
prismatic flickering light
hidden in the day
as we bask in its rays
the flame is a hunger
driving against the night
I fear its all-encompassing tongues
dancing within my heart and tongue

→

as they bless and quench
our soul-driven search
for each other in the days and our nights
you are my pillar of fire
like the Israelites
like the birds we take flight
you, oh guide
holy burning angel of delight.

Wash me clean with your dark
brown eyes' gaze of love and mercy,
my lord of silence, light and play.
Sulfur hues of gold, green and blues,
le maitre de feu d'or et bleu,
the rising sky-driven swath,
beckons me to walk and fly with you
on its God-given path
eliciting rays from my heart
the tender sound of your name
flickering from the sparks and tips
of the flame
a burning log always changing,
always remaining the same
warming us with its deep replies of love
soul's sustenance, soul consequence
spellbinding, life-changing game
of love and death.

Singing to a Sea of Faces

Applause floods the room
like crackling waves of
white water fences
blurring so many faces,
the spotlight on my sequined jacket dances.
I travel through the throng
by the swing of my gavel
to fill the theatre's night with song.
It is the singer's road I travel
to harness the energy of dreams
by a song's greatness I'm touched
and the madness that I won't amount to much.
Standing on the edge
of a stage of lights and darkness
without a crutch
just my voice, hands and heart
and this hunch
singing to a sea of faces
looking to make it all appear
as coincidence and luck.

The overwhelming night of the senses
blurs so many faces with fences.
They were made by me so that I'd be freed
from my anxiety.
Self-yoking, I travel
by the swing of my gavel

to block out the night,
harness the energies of dreams
and touched by madness
I won't amount to much.
But I want to dream of nothing else
but stand on the edge
of a stage of lights and darkness
without a crutch
just my voice, hands and heart
singing to a sea of faces
and make it all appear
as coincidence and luck.

The Jungle

Blessed are the poor
blessed are the meek
rip roaring drunk
through the jungle we peek.
Through the trees and bushes,
stepping over fallen logs
I seek the fallen rainbow,
the hidden promise
from so long ago.
I yearn to touch your hand,
feel it touching mine
with prolonged intensity
connecting
the me and the you
instead of lying here alone
herded into a green waste
I keep thinking I have outgrown.
But the jungle always remains.
This one has my name on it.
Uncleared it looks the same
until I enter it, meekly again
and embrace its silent awe.
The jungle lives in me
hidden in my core.

Poems on a Train to Albany

I

I admit I have no undertaking
      that's so great.
I admit that I could be more alive
      to present circumstance.
I concede that your voice
      is uncontainable,
greater than the winds
      and surf that
upon the shoreline dies.

Yet I wonder
      if you'll hear my muffled weeping
and my stark confusion in
      hidden voices tucked inside.

Narcissus' wandering transfixed
      in a mirrored pool
unmoving
      silent as stone
and just as sharp
      as razor-edged cliffs
I throw myself upon
      when they try to come near
and others are dashed to invisible bits.

II

Why not life
        as I find my voice, but
how will I listen for your refraction?

You permeate all
        you are
beneath the deepest depths
        and I want to touch you
and rise
        with each ounce
of silent
        rising
breath.
        Breath bestowed
undying, brash and bold
        bountiful fruits of the earth
shoot through the soil
        green leaves and flowers
reach to the sky.
        Always a question
before they die
        why not life?

III

I follow your shadow...
        and I cannot fathom
how deep you want me to go.
        Your shadow is light

→

despite the heavy shadows that
      stain and hide my life.
You are always with me
      inexplicably why
we stay together as partners and lovers despite
      the hiding of passion met stars,
veils waiting to be torn away
      with my secret depression and mistrust.
I want you forever
      and you continue racing after me
though lately I think you are always
      standing still.
How long will it take me
      to believe it?
How long will my will
      remain immutable, impenetrable
before I take the final leap of faith,
      shatter my illusions and
allow my heart be filled?

Museum

The Entrance and the Great Hall
Up the broad staircase
through columns of stone,
you stroll into the Great Hall
so small within these halls of fate,
dwarfed by time's achievements.
One is always arriving late.
Though walking with others,
in these walls of history and stone
somehow, you feel you've
strolled in alone.

The tri-domed cupola ceiling
high above milling visitors.
with maps or audio devices,
Muses fly through the great hall
chafing like stallions, ready to bolt.
or galloping wildly,
at the entrance they halt,
for they cannot leave the vault
perched in their bell towers,
voices echoing through staircases
fly directly at you,
like Zeus' lightning bolt.

To entrance you, they sing;
as you bring your curiosity

from the lighted ceilings
to the centuries that fly
past time and relics of the past enshrined.

They tell of journeys beyond these halls
they roam for miles to find their home.
Through medieval cities and castles,
while caravans of camels cross deserts
irrigated by the Nile.

Nomads call out and sing
searching for their homelands.
So go the aching tales of woe
and hopeful dreams of mirth

The Egyptian Section
World of silent stone
ages tell how dreams are sown
amid shadows
softened dark caresses.
Massive walls
bathed in muted light recessed
the crevices of hidden passages,
the hollow chamber,
a slumbering sarcophagus.

On the walls of a tomb
hieroglyphs encode
for the pharaoh god to travel across the sky
magic incantations wide

carry the royal chosen soul of the earth
in his immortal Sun-boat.
He who once breathed upon the cool night
in the Valley of the Kings
now lies beneath the dark descending night
in a desert of sighs.

Hall of Greek and Roman Antiquities
Marbled Greek figures mute,
the last stilled reflections of a Roman head,
so alive, so astute
in homage to the dead.
Perhaps it is Cicero
speaking on the senate floor from his urgent tome.
Most now is lost but his greatness is forever
dreamed into stone.

Apollo plays upon his lyre
on a vase, black and red afire.
Bracelets, necklaces and rings,
faded jewels once gleaming bright,
adorned ladies walking,
their torches blazing,
a solemn procession in the night.
Vases cradled in the arms of slaves
traveling through the city
Vendors' wares waxened with age,
encased and dwarfed by passers-by,
oddly devoid of curiosity, or pity.

→

The Temple of Dendur

Mammoth walls beneath a sky-lit lean-to
upon a raised dais, reclined.
The light falls in existential softness,
a macrocosm of light and shades
and centuries of worn warm limestone
lapping up time.

The Chinese Garden

Garden of water welling
struck up from silence depths.
Frozen rock formations spilling
suspended into volcanic rock shaped clefts.
Time waits here for drinking
below the atrium square's
Chinese tiled gabled roof.
Beneath the skylight:
staring white softness
like a cloudy white lit day,
overcast.
My spirit welling
waits to rise
and sing,
caressed
by this watery remembrance
of my origin
evoked and rushedly ravished,
its evocation hushed
by a fountain,
and a pool.

Picasso's Room: The Three Sisters

The shudder of canvas to paint,
drying paint to light.
Colors rescue the world from dreariness;
frowns, anger and spite
spew forth for an unvoiced sigh
fired from envisioning within
as it dries.

***

Creation blazes forth
in the museum where
it longs for all its due.
Time to uproot the silent,
plant in the wonder of being
sightseeing present's past
anew.

Snow White

Snow White doesn't live here anymore.
She was banished for eating apples.
Now we have a new order entering:
the sorrowful dwarfs kneel
before their sleeping princess
keeping watch with sharp chagrin
countenances helpless, tearful, grim.

Forests have been done away with (burnt).
The rivers' bridges are all laid with tracks,
while the skies are filled with planes.
The horses have lost their manes.
Royalty is gone,
the Church is decaying within
its ancient shrines.
The proletariat has boiled over,
crowds upturned Lenin's tomb.
The refusal to use birth control has frozen
over the mothers' wombs
into a vagina monologue.

The football teams are attacking the hockey players
with their own sticks
as they run towards the moon.
The sun is summoning spring to
peek its head out too soon.

And I am stuck trying
too heavy to sing,
too light to spring,
caught somewhere, somehow
in between
the highs and the lows
of singing solo
and duet
with somebody.

Mercury Pausing

Marble lined
echoes in the halls of white
dark hued statuesque figures still
the mercurial figure in bronze
gazing at his message,
a memory dearly bought
from one fair Zeus.

Nature's Force

Force is a current of nature
meant to fly like passion's flow
beyond controlling lives
igniting the fusion of fiery spirits'
unharnessed tides.
And so, the electricity goes
when pressed and aged like wine:
the bottle uncorked
at just the right time
as the table is set
and guests are finally seated
when the host has given the sign.
Dinner is slowly served
to soothe all your ills,
and turn the dissonance of waiting
into rhyme.

Enlightening and lightening,
imbibing this solemn moment's peak.
Spurred on by memory
of the golden hallowed past
and the future we let speak.

→

Sparked on by memory
and nature's pull
towards oneness and the all
close to love's silent meal filled.
Silently, single-mindedly
delightfully magical;
ever full.

Xochimilco's Waters

Towards the zenith of opportunity
we take flight.
In spite of numbing
torn despairing dreams
we ignite.

Soaring on wingéd air
soaring unhindered where
we (are in flight) alight
beating our wings
keeping those dreams from mooring
earning the right
to fly through
creation's depths and height.

We take flight.
We take flight.
We take flight.

Into unknown depths
feeling paths of sight,
that led us to one path
together, sharing time

caressing tender joy
still young,
still shining bright.

→

A calm of silent stillness
stilled in the floating afternoon
on Xochimilco's ships of flowers,
birds speeding over the waters,
lightly skipping
the rustling water's waves.

Christmas Eve
(where the Self is restored)

I used to cite the Holy Scriptures
make their incantations speak
repressing
incandescent
unconscious
undulations of speech
deemed too self-indulgent
and never within my reach.
I despised myself for being
tremulous
too tender
too weak.

Still, I continued my search for the Lamb
and the right to speak
beyond tunnel blinded journeying
with the Magi's gifts
walking the sands of silent time
on this very starlit night at peace
no longer anxious
no longer blind
no longer yearning for surcease.

Now my clumsy cooling star shines
no longer waiting to be changed
like water into wine

➝

my heart awakened
held up to the light
warmed for the night
where long ago,
I took up my Egyptian flight
to join with others
where holding I was held
the Self was restored.
Consciousness was transformed.
My time reveled!

Compelled
to grow with boldness,
shake off the dullness of weary sleep,
wanton woundedness
spun into a cocoon
of waiting dreamless darkness
so deep.

About the Poet

Kevin Clifford Burke is a poet and musician. He is the author of two books of poetry entitled: *Angry June Moon Says Hello: Poems To Come Out To* (2010) and *The Bridge of Love* (2011). The author is a psychoanalyst and psychotherapist in private practice who is also associated with The Training Institute for Mental Health in New York City as a Senior Supervisor. Mr. Burke has also worked in the child welfare field for over 30 years and is currently a managing supervisor in NYC Children's Services. Mr. Burke and Miguel, his husband and partner of thirty-six years, reside in Staten Island, NY. The author is also a cabaret performer, a singer/songwriter and classical guitarist who has been performing regularly in cabaret venues for over a decade.

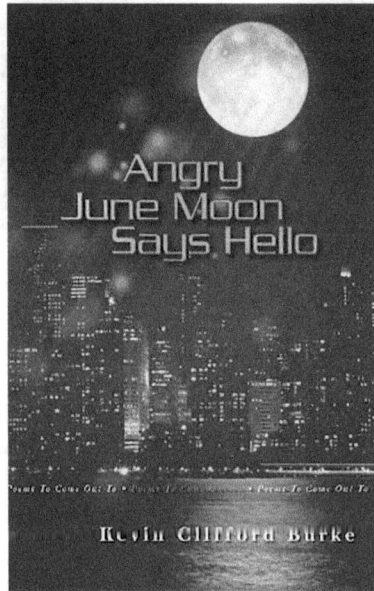

Angry June Moon Says Hello:
Poems To Come Out To

Kevin Clifford Burke

These autobiographical poems trace my journey of coming out as a gay man over a period of twenty-six years. They are infused with my own unique lyrical voice and spiritual visions, enriched with rhythmic musicality, rhyme, heart wrenching poignancy and intimate vulnerability.

"Angry June Moon Says Hello is an invigorating collection... which resonates through emotionally loaded hymns about ethereal and human experience... Reverberating through each poem are allusions to mythology and religion, popular culture, and the natural environment."

Burke cleverly plays with literal and figurative mediums to draw out his arduous philosophy...His "enriching lyric therefore pays homage to a demographic otherwise silenced by mainstream, heterosexual culture...and "serves as a didactic touchstone in heeding thresholds of human compliancy for a man in search of self-preservation..."

San Francisco Book Review (Erienne Rojas January 8, 2011)

ISBN: 1439265798, ISBN-13: 9781439265796

85 pages, soft cover

12.95

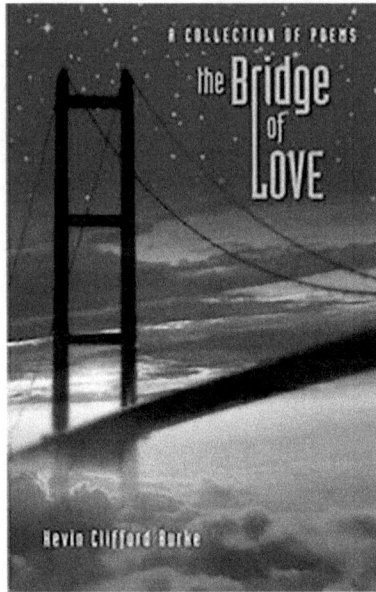

The Bridge of Love
A Collection of Poems
Kevin Clifford Burke

"Kevin Clifford Burke's poetry collection, *The Bridge of Love*, asks readers to take risks, live in the moment, and love without hesitation. These themes are skillfully threaded through the collection. The universal nature of the poems make them well-suited for readers looking for inspiration and hope in a world full of chaos. Similarly, the poems' rich sound play, beautiful metaphors, and lyrical wrangling will reel in poetry enthusiasts."

Lisa Bower (2011)
ForeWord Clarion Review

ISBN: 1452836493, ISBN-13: 9781452836492, LCCN: 2010906123
36 pages, soft cover
12.95

Acknowledgements

Martin Keefe is the author of two novels: Taking the Measure and Tales from a Cardboard Box.

Howard J Kogan is a retired psychotherapist and writer. His two books of poetry, "Indian Summer" and "A Chill in the Air" are available from the publisher, Square Circle Press and Amazon, his novel, "No View" is available from Amazon (Kindle or print).

John McCaffrey is the author of a novel and two collections of short stories. His latest book, Automatically Hip, another collection, will be released in July 2022. John is also a creative writing teacher, helps to direct a nonprofit organization in New York City, and is a weekly columnist for The Good Men Project. jamccaffrey.com

www.ingramcontent.com/pod-product-compliance
Lightning Source LLC
LaVergne TN
LVHW021616080426
835510LV00019B/2605